VIKINGS

by Martin Gitlin

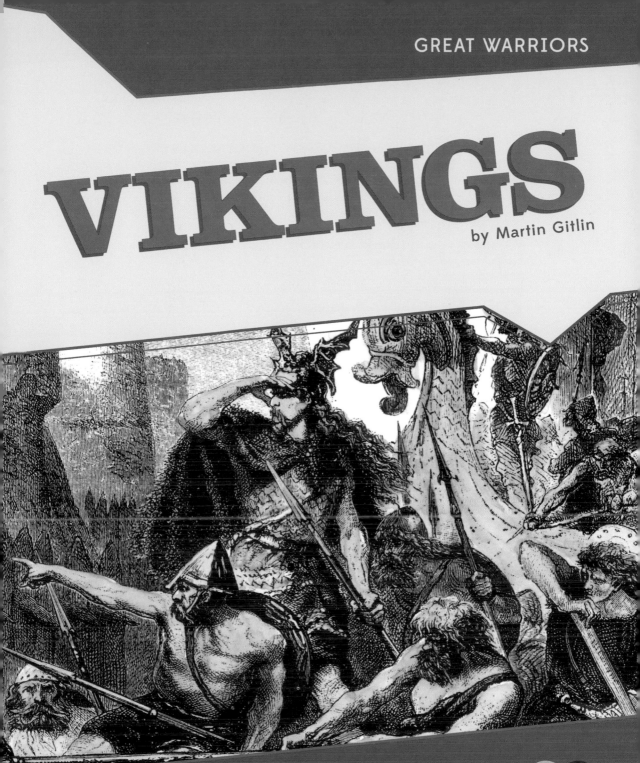

Content Consultant
Scott A. Mellor
Distinguished Lecturer, Department of Scandinavian
Studies, University of Wisconsin–Madison

CORE
LIBRARY

Published by ABDO Publishing Company, PO Box 398166, Minneapolis, MN 55439. Copyright © 2013 by Abdo Consulting Group, Inc. International copyrights reserved in all countries. No part of this book may be reproduced in any form without written permission from the publisher. The Core Library™ is a trademark and logo of ABDO Publishing Company.

Printed in the United States of America,
North Mankato, Minnesota
102012
012013
♻ THIS BOOK CONTAINS AT LEAST 10% RECYCLED MATERIALS.

Editor: Lauren Coss
Series Designer: Becky Daum

Library of Congress Cataloging-in-Publication Data
Gitlin, Martin.
 Vikings / Martin Gitlin.
   p. cm. -- (Great warriors)
Includes bibliographical references and index.
ISBN 978-1-61783-729-6
1. Vikings--Juvenile literature. 2. Explorers--Juvenile literature. 1. Title.
948.02--dc22
                                        2012946373

Photo Credits: North Wind/North Wind Picture Archives, cover, 1, 13, 14, 20, 32, 40; Thinkstock, 4, 7, 28, 45; Lindisfarne Priory Museum/English Heritage, 8; Frits Solvang/Dorling Kindersley, 10; Everett Collection/Shutterstock Images, 17; Red Line Editorial, 18; Dorling Kindersley, 23; iStockphoto, 26, 36; Shutterstock Images, 31; Nigel Hicks/Dorling Kindersley, 35; Archive Photos/Getty Images, 38

CONTENTS

CHAPTER ONE

MAYHEM ON A HOLY ISLAND

It was a windy day on the island of Lindisfarne in northern England. Lightning flashed across the sky. The ominous weather seemed to warn of danger ahead.

It was January 8, 793. Families living in the village were going about their daily business. Monks were working quietly in the island's monastery. Nobody on Lindisfarne knew that off the east coast of the island,

Viking raiders destroyed the Lindisfarne monastery in 793. Tourists can still visit the ruins of the monastery.

A Ship for a Long Trip

A Viking ship from before the 700s could not have survived the long journey to England. Sails on these ships were too small to sail long distances. Eventually the Vikings used longships. These ships had oars and a much larger sail. Longships were also better able to handle rough seas. By 793 this improved construction, including advancements to the ships' keels, allowed the Vikings to make the journey to Lindisfarne safely.

a great Viking ship was racing toward the shore. Wooden Viking ships with sails and oars were among the strongest and fastest in the world.

Up to No Good

Later that day, the sailors brought mayhem to the island. They were there to find riches and people to use for slave labor.

The Vikings slaughtered sheep and oxen. They killed priests and nuns. They burned the monastery. They murdered or captured church workers. They dragged some islanders into the ocean and drowned them. Then they sailed away with new slaves and ships full of gold and jewelry from the monastery.

Most European boats would not have survived the voyage through the cold northern seas. But Viking ships were the best in Europe.

The First of Many Raids

The Vikings lived in a violent time. Cultural groups across Europe were launching deadly attacks on one another to acquire resources and land. The brutal Lindisfarne attack was no exception. It was like many the Vikings carried out during this period. But although they used combat to acquire resources, many Vikings were also peaceful farmers and traders.

Before the Lindisfarne raid, most Europeans saw Vikings as traders rather than raiders. Vikings

The Lindisfarne Stone

The Lindisfarne Stone is believed to be a depiction of the Viking raid in 793. One side shows seven warriors. What does this stone tell you about the Lindisfarne raid? Look closely at the warriors' clothing and weapons. How does this compare to the description of the raid in this chapter?

were trade partners with nations as far south as the Mediterranean Sea. But overpopulation and a lack of resources at home led the Vikings to pillage rather than trade. Vikings soon began seeking new sources of wealth through conquests in other countries.

The raid on Lindisfarne was the first recorded major Viking attack on England. But it was certainly not the last. The Vikings had started on a path of destruction that would last for centuries. The British people soon learned more about the Viking warriors.

English writer Simeon of Durham described the tragedy at Lindisfarne in the following passage from his *History of the Kings of England*:

> The pagans from the northern regions came with a naval force to Britain like stinging hornets and spread on all sides like fearful wolves, robbed, tore and slaughtered not only beasts of burden, sheep and oxen, but even priests and deacons, and companies of monks and nuns.
>
> And they came to the church at Lindisfarne, laid everything waste with grievous plundering, trampled the holy places with polluted steps, dug up the altars and seized all the treasures of the holy church. They killed some of the brothers, took some away with them in fetters, many they drove out, naked and loaded with insults, some they drowned in the sea.

Source: Robert Ferguson. *The Vikings. New York: Viking Penguin*, 2009. Print. 42.

What's the Big Idea?

Take a close look at Simeon of Durham's words. What is his main idea? What evidence does he use to support his point? Come up with a short paragraph showing how Simeon of Durham uses two or three pieces of evidence to support a main point.

CHAPTER TWO

VIKING WARRIORS SET SAIL

Vikings were Scandinavian warriors, pirates, and traders. The first recorded mentions of a word similar to *Viking* were found in Old English poems. The word meant "sea warriors." The term was viewed as an insult at the time, so most Vikings probably did not refer to themselves as Vikings.

A museum in Oslo, Norway, houses a reconstructed Viking longship.

Vikings came from the coastal regions of Scandinavia, which included the countries of Norway, Sweden, and Denmark. The population was divided into clans, usually led by a chieftain. Sometimes Vikings arrived quietly in other countries. They built peaceful settlements in places such as Iceland, Greenland, and Canada. But some Viking warriors violently attacked other nations. In these cases, they were looking for valuables and the resources they needed to survive.

Vikings and Your Vocabulary

The Viking invaders brought the Old Norse language to England. As a result, many English words spoken today have Old Norse roots. Among them are "cast" (*kasta*), "knife" (*knifr*), "take" (*taka*), "window" (*vind-auga*), "egg" (*egg*), "ill" (*illr*), "them" (*theim*), and "die" (*deyja*).

Expanding Their Horizons

Viking warriors first sailed to England. They knew monasteries often stored money and valuable objects. They followed their attack on Lindisfarne with raids on other

Holy places, such as monasteries, had little security and few defenses. They were often located on small islands. As a result, they were prime targets for Viking raids.

English and French monasteries. They also attacked trading centers close to shore to steal valuables. Early Viking raids used small fleets of warriors. These groups made surprise raids on unsuspecting towns. It was a new style of warfare. The victims had little defense.

In their homelands, Vikings faced overpopulation and a lack of resources. Soon the Vikings began coming to foreign lands in much larger numbers. In some raids, as many as 350 ships sped ashore. Once they arrived, Vikings plundered, killed, and took

Viking raiders sail down the River Seine and into Paris in the late 800s.

slaves. They also began settling their seized lands. The Vikings soon created colonies in parts of England and France. They also took over parts of Ireland and Russia.

They were just getting started. In 845 Viking raiders led by Ragnar Lodbrok overran Paris, France. Some European rulers even tried paying the Vikings to leave. Viking warriors across Europe were capturing more and more new territory. By 866 they had established a kingdom in York, England. Their force in England was known as the Great Army.

Ruthless Raider

Some Vikings were tricky as well as violent. In the early 860s, the Viking Hastein and his men wanted to attack the Italian town of Luna. But Hastein believed the town's defenses were too strong. He came up with a plan. Hastein's men told the people of Luna their Viking chief was dead. The Italians agreed to allow the Vikings into their town to bury their leader. The Vikings walked sadly to the grave site carrying Hastein in a coffin. Once inside the town, Hastein jumped out of the coffin. He then led a rampage through the streets.

Moving In

Some leaders willingly gave Vikings sections of their countries. They hoped by doing so, Vikings would choose to let their citizens live in peace. In 911 French king Charles the Simple made a deal with Vikings. He gave them an area of France called Normandy. In return Viking leader Rollo became a Christian and supported Charles. Rollo defended Normandy against other Viking attacks. In 954 the Viking king of the York kingdom was overthrown. His defeat ended the first Viking Age.

But Viking warriors were not done spreading their mayhem in England. In the late 900s, the second Viking Age began. These Vikings were more organized. By the 1000s, few Viking chieftains were left. Powerful Scandinavian kings led entire countries. Instead of small attacks, these powerful royal leaders planned large-scale raids. They expanded Viking territory beyond Scandinavia. The armies of Danish king Sweyn Forkbeard and son Canute carried out

This modern copy of a Viking longship features fierce carvings, just like ancient Viking ships. The carvings were designed to frighten the Vikings' victims.

new attacks on English towns in 1013. They destroyed every town they came across. They captured prisoners as they went.

Sweyn's armies ran into heavy resistance in London. They traveled along the Thames River. Eventually they seized the western section of England. Soon British king Ethelred was driven from his throne. Sweyn became king of England. Sweyn died in 1014, and the Vikings named Canute as his replacement in 1016.

Viking Territory

From the 700s to the 1000s, Vikings spread their territory far and wide. This map shows some of the major Viking colonies. What does this map tell you about Viking expansion? Using the map and the information in this chapter, write a short paragraph explaining how the Vikings settled the territory shown on the map.

Canute became king of Denmark and England, and he made use of his power. Eventually Canute and his allies overthrew Norwegian king Olaf Haraldsson. Canute was one of the most powerful and respected rulers of his time. His rule in England improved trade with other countries. He had a good relationship with the Roman emperor and the pope. He used these friendships to help England. He put English citizens in positions of power. Vikings had earned their violent reputation, but Canute's rule was largely a time of peace for England.

FURTHER EVIDENCE

There was quite a bit of information about Viking warriors in Chapter Two. It covered battles and campaigns over a period of almost 300 years. But if you could pick out the main point of the chapter, what would it be? Visit the Web site below to learn more about Viking battles. Choose a quote from the Web site that relates to this chapter. Write a few sentences explaining how the quote you found relates to this chapter.

Vikings
www.history.com/topics/vikings

WEAPONS, TOOLS, AND WAYS OF WAR

A Viking ship was a terrifying sight. A huge carved dragon often stood out in front. Blood-red sails flapped in the wind. People throughout Europe had heard stories of these warriors' brutality. One glimpse of a Viking warship offshore was enough to terrify anyone in its path.

Early Viking attacks were based on speed. Vikings arrived by ship quickly and with weapons ready for

Viking ships could carry as many as 100 Vikings.

Swords

Many Viking warriors carried swords. A sword was a symbol of high status. Viking swords were often coated with silver or copper. The weapons often had detailed decorations. These gave information about the sword's owner. Warriors even gave their swords names. Swords were sometimes passed down from father to son for many generations. Many swords were buried alongside Viking owners who had died.

action. This gave their enemies little time to prepare a defense. Vikings took what prisoners and valuables they could from the town. Then the warriors returned to their ships and sailed away.

Weapons and Armor

Movies often show Viking warriors wearing horned helmets. Real-life Viking helmets were likely made of leather. A helmet often had a piece of metal at the bridge of the nose or near the eyes for extra protection.

The Vikings dressed for warmth and flexibility in battle. Like most people at the time, they wore tunics. Leather jackets covered the tunics. Sometimes

Many Viking warriors fought with swords.

they wore mail, or shirts made of iron fabric. The mail helped protect a Viking in combat. But it was also very heavy. According to stories, many Vikings left their mail on the ship. They did not want to be weighed down during raids.

The Vikings' main weapon was the battle-ax. It could be used in hand-to-hand combat or thrown at the enemy. Some Viking warriors used iron swords.

The Berserkirs

The English phrase "going berserk" means to commit mayhem. The words can be traced to a mythical Viking named Tyr. Tyr wore a bearskin cloak and used a bear's head as a helmet. Warriors training for battle wearing bearskin clothing were called *berserkirs*. The berserkirs prepared for battle by working themselves into a frenzy, which got them excited to fight.

Others carried spears and knives. They carried round shields for protection. By 1000, Vikings were using long, kite-shaped shields. These shields protected the Vikings' legs when they were fighting.

A New Strategy

As European defenses got better, their shipbuilding skills improved. Their goals were to use ships for both trade and battle.

Europeans soon were able to battle attacking Viking ships near the shore.

Viking leaders responded by changing their tactics. They moved from small raids to large attacks. They created large and powerful armies. In some raids, as many as 200 warships sailed to European targets. Vikings established permanent settlements in these foreign lands for security. Their large armies were able to dominate their enemies.

Bands of Viking warriors usually broke up after military campaigns ended. Sometimes they joined other warrior bands. Other Vikings returned home to their lives as farmers, salesmen, or craftsmen.

EXPLORE ONLINE

The focus in Chapter Three was Viking weapons and strategies of war. It also touched on clothing that Viking warriors wore in combat. The British Web site below focuses on the same subjects. As you know, every source is different. How is the information given on the British Web site different from the information in this chapter? What can you learn from this Web site?

Viking Weapons and Warfare
www.bbc.co.uk/history/ancient/vikings/weapons_01.shtml

CHAPTER FOUR

GODS, MYTHS, AND LEGENDS

Viking mythology inspired many in the ancient Scandinavian world. It especially influenced the mighty Viking warriors who overran Europe.

The Vikings worshipped many gods with mystical powers. They told stories about their gods. The stories were not written down, but rather shared by telling them over and over. The stories carried

Scandinavian poets known as skalds shared Viking history and mythology.

Thor's hammer was said to return to him after each time he threw it.

messages and inspiration and helped the Vikings make sense of their world.

The most important god to kings and chieftains was Odin. He was the god of war and poetry. Norse mythology claimed Odin lived in Valhalla, a mythical mansion for slain Viking warriors. Viking warriors believed they were destined for Valhalla after they were killed in battle.

Another legendary Viking god of war was Odin's powerful son, Thor. He carried a hammer called Mjollnir. Thor battled giants but was kind and generous to humans.

More Gods

Norse mythology had many gods besides Odin and Thor. Among the other gods in Old Norse mythology were Freyr and his sister, Freyja.

Viking Worlds

Vikings saw their universe as a flat circle. This circle was divided into several parts. Asgard was at the center of the circle. This was the world of the gods, including Odin, Thor, and Freyja. Midgard, the home of the humans, encircled Asgard.

Freyr was one of the most celebrated of all gods during the Viking Age. He was a god of fertility and birth. He was also associated with the rain and sun. Farmers called upon him for fertile crops in the spring. Newlyweds asked him to bless them with many children.

Freyr's sister, Freyja, was a goddess of love, fertility, battle, and death. She represented female power. She took half of the slain warriors to her great hall. The other half went with Odin to Valhalla.

The Big, Bad Wolf

According to Viking mythology, Loki's son was a wolf named Fenrir. Fenrir was so powerful he frightened the other gods. The gods tricked him into tying himself up with a magical chain. Eventually, Fenrir will break free and swallow Odin, which will destroy the world.

Loki was a god of mischief and lies. He was the son of giants. Like the rest of the gods, he had the power to change shape. He enjoyed playing tricks on the other gods.

The Borgund Stave Church in Norway was likely built in the late 1100s and is still standing today.

Turning to Christianity

Over time some Vikings who settled outside Scandinavia adopted Christianity as their religion. English and German missionaries sometimes arrived in Scandinavia to convert Vikings and other Scandinavians to Christianity. Some Vikings brought the religion back to their Scandinavian homes. By the 1000s, most people in Denmark and Norway had converted to Christianity. In the 1100s, Sweden became a Christian nation.

CHAPTER FIVE

EXPLORING NEW WORLDS

By the early 1000s, Scandinavians had explored and set up colonies in many places across the world. Most Vikings were now settled permanently in lands they had taken over. They had established settlements in Iceland, Greenland, and across Europe. By the mid-1000s, there were few Viking raids.

Christopher Columbus often receives credit as the first European to arrive in North America. But Leif Eriksson and other Viking explorers beat Columbus by almost 500 years.

Some explorers in the Viking Age were especially adventurous. These Scandinavians sailed westward into unknown lands. The first such explorer was Ingólfur Arnarson. Ingólfur and his foster brother, Leif Hrodmarsson, were found guilty of murder. They decided to flee their home country.

In 874 the two began their journey west on separate ships. They brought their wives, slaves, cattle, crew, and everything else they owned. Soon they reached the island today known as Iceland. There they went their separate ways.

The slaves soon killed Leif and his men. Ingólfur fared better. A few years after arriving in Iceland, Ingólfur built a

Horrible Harald

Many historians believe Iceland was settled because of Norway's brutal king in the 800s. Many Norwegians viewed King Harald Fairhair as a cruel leader. He turned many of his citizens into slaves. People who tried to resist him were often killed or forced to flee the country. Many of those who left traveled west to the tiny island of Iceland.

A statue of Ingólfur Arnarson still stands in Reykjavik, Iceland.

new settlement. Ingólfur's settlement is now known as Reykjavik, the capital city of Iceland. Soon more Norse and Celtic settlers arrived in Reykjavik. The settlers raised sheep. They used the island's natural resources to make weapons, pots, and clothing.

Going to Greenland

Among the 10,000 Scandinavian settlers in Iceland was a Norwegian Viking named Erik Thorvaldsson.

Viking explorers were some of the first Scandinavians to settle along Greenland's coasts.

He was known as Erik the Red, probably because of the color of his hair. Erik the Red had a violent temper. He killed two men after an argument. He was banished from Iceland for three years as punishment.

In 982 he fled westward with his family. He soon reached a large island. The land was cold and icy. Little of it was farmable. But Erik the Red named the island Greenland. He believed the name would encourage settlers from Iceland to move there.

Erik the Red settled in southwestern Greenland. He returned to Iceland in 986 to share his discovery. He convinced many Icelanders to join him. These colonists settled areas of the southern and western coasts. They built farms on the edges of fjords. They herded sheep and cattle, and they ate reindeer and seal. By 1000 there were approximately 1,000 Scandinavians living in Greenland.

On to North America

The Vikings continued pushing westward. Sometime around the year 986, Bjarni Herjulfsson set out from Greenland for Iceland. But on the journey, his ship blew off course. Bjarni landed far away in an unknown territory. Historians today believe he reached the eastern coast of Canada.

Bjarni returned to Greenland. He told a curious Leif Eriksson, Erik the Red's son, about his incredible journey. Leif decided to find this unknown land. Around the year 1000, he set sail to the south and west. He landed on an island he called Vinland in 1001.

Thorvald and other Viking Age explorers did not always get along with the Native Americans already living in North America.

Scholars believe Vinland was the modern-day Canadian province of Newfoundland and Labrador. Leif's group explored Vinland and built some houses. Later, another group of Vikings led by Leif's brother Thorvald sailed to Vinland. Thorvald soon died in a fight with Native Americans, but his group lived there for several years. Eventually they abandoned the settlement and returned to Greenland.

End of the Viking Age

Vinland was the final major settlement of Viking explorers. The European world was changing at this time. Many Scandinavians had converted to Christianity, which did not support the violent Viking raids. Scandinavians were less concerned with armies and raiding. They could now make money more easily by trading.

In 1066 Norwegian king Harald Sigurdsson attempted to invade England. He was killed fighting English king Harold Godwinson in the Battle of Stamford Bridge. This was the last major Viking invasion. Godwinson died three weeks later in the Battle

Leif's Neighbors

Humans had been living in Vinland long before Vikings arrived. The natives in the area were known as *Skraelings*. At first the Vikings and Skraelings cooperated with each other. They were trade partners. But soon the relationship turned sour. The Skraelings eventually forced the Vikings to return to Greenland. Occasionally Vikings returned to North America for timber, but they never lived there again.

William the Conqueror defeated the English king and his army in the Battle of Hastings.

of Hastings against William the Conqueror. William was from Normandy, part of northern France. He introduced Norman culture across England. The age of the Vikings was over.

Vikings left a powerful impression on Europe and the world. One thousand years later, people still remember them and try to understand their ways. The modern world remains fascinated by their military conquests, mythology, and spirit of adventure.

The Viking Age was a violent time. Viking Egill Skallagrimsson wrote the following poem about his time as a warrior around the year 925. The poem was later discovered on a rune stone, a raised stone with an inscription.

I've been with sword and spear

slippery with bright blood

where kites wheeled. And how well

we violent Vikings clashed!

Red flames ate up men's roofs,

raging we killed and killed,

and skewered bodies sprawled

sleepy in town gate-ways

Source: Else Roesdahl. The Vikings. *New York: Penguin Books, 1998. Print. 145–146.*

Nice View

After reading this poem, go back and reread the Simeon of Durham's passage in Chapter One. How does the poem shed new light on Simeon's writing? What is the point of view of each author? How are these two authors' points of view similar? How are they different? Write a short essay comparing the two points of view reflected in the primary sources in this book.

IMPORTANT DATES AND BATTLES

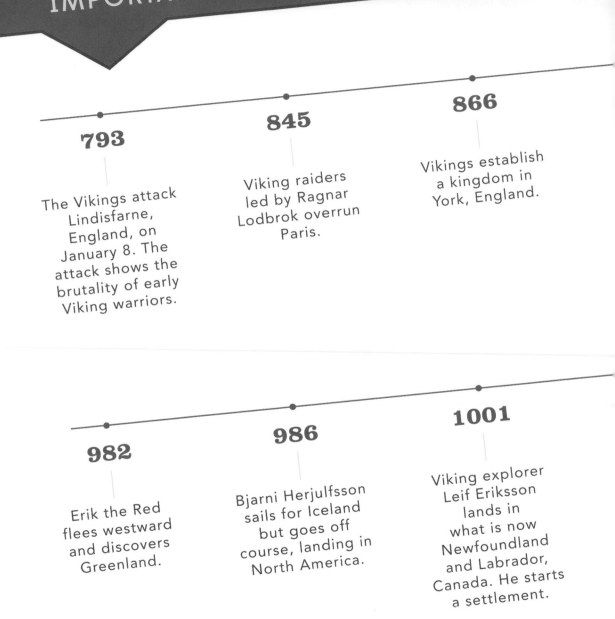

793

The Vikings attack Lindisfarne, England, on January 8. The attack shows the brutality of early Viking warriors.

845

Viking raiders led by Ragnar Lodbrok overrun Paris.

866

Vikings establish a kingdom in York, England.

982

Erik the Red flees westward and discovers Greenland.

986

Bjarni Herjulfsson sails for Iceland but goes off course, landing in North America.

1001

Viking explorer Leif Eriksson lands in what is now Newfoundland and Labrador, Canada. He starts a settlement.

874

Ingólfur Arnarson and Leif Hrodmarsson begin their journey to Iceland.

911

Charles the Simple gives Viking Rollo the land of Normandy in 911. Rollo protects the country from other Vikings.

954

The fall of the York kingdom marks the end of the first Viking Age.

1013

Danish king Forkbeard and son Canute begin new attacks on England.

1016

Canute becomes king of Denmark and England. Soon he controls Norway too.

1066

English King Harold Godwinson is slain. William the Conqueror and his Normans take over. The Viking Age ends.

Why Do I Care?

The Viking Age ended almost 1,000 years ago. But that doesn't mean you can't find similarities between your life and the world of Viking warriors. How does the Viking Age affect your life today? Are there words or traditions that might not exist without them? How might your life be different if the Vikings had never come into power? Use your imagination!

Another View

There are many sources online and in your library about the Vikings. Ask a librarian or another adult to help you find a reliable source on the Vikings. Compare what you learn in this new source to what you have found out in this book. Then write a short essay comparing and contrasting the new source's view of the Vikings with the ideas in this book. How are they different? How are they similar? Why do you think they are different or similar?

Surprise Me

The history and culture of the Vikings can be interesting and surprising. What two or three facts about the Vikings did you find most surprising? Write a few sentences about each fact. Why did you find them surprising?

Say What?

Learning about the Vikings can mean learning a lot of new vocabulary. Can you find five words in this book you've never seen or heard? First find out the meanings of those words. Then write down the meanings in your own words. After that try to use each word in a new sentence.

GLOSSARY

brutal
especially cruel

campaign
a series of battles to achieve
a goal

chieftain
the leader of a band or a clan

colony
a group of people who form
a settlement in a new land

convert
convince someone to adopt a
particular religion

fjord
a long, narrow inlet of the sea
bordered by cliffs

mayhem
random acts of violence and
damage

monastery
a secluded home occupied
by monks who have taken
religious vows

Norse
Scandinavian people or
language

pillage
steal in battle

plunder
steal by force

tunic
a long shirt often worn as
part of a military uniform

LEARN MORE

Books

Chrisp, Peter. *Strange Histories: The Vikings.* Chicago: Raintree, 2003.

Kimmel, Elizabeth Cody. *Before Columbus: The Leif Eriksson Expedition.* New York: Random House Books, 2003.

Schaffer, David. *The Viking Conquest.* San Diego: Lucent Books, 2002.

Web Links

To learn more about Viking warriors, visit ABDO Publishing Company online at **www.abdopublishing.com.** Web sites about Viking warriors are featured on our Book Links page. These links are routinely monitored and updated to provide the most current information available.

Visit **www.mycorelibrary.com** for free additional tools for teachers and students.

INDEX

ABOUT THE AUTHOR

Martin Gitlin is a freelance writer based in Cleveland, Ohio. He has written more than 60 educational books. Gitlin has won more than 45 awards during his 30 years as a writer, including first place for general excellence from the Associated Press. He lives with his wife and three children.